The Clone in Me

Samuel Rain Benjamin

I0677891

Complicated Passions

Private Collection

Written, edited & formatted by Samuel Rain Benjamin

Everybody Publishing/Long Beach, California

Take Me

This is my love like I said I would be
beyond these words
I'll be the Man you need

sharing these sensual pleasures
my dare whispering your name

taste this recipe
in all the right places
and have it like your dreams

before & after:

Dark Man Blues:

If I knew love I would call her

make it my confession

just to confess

my dreams

whispering how temptation

dared me

how my emotions

made me

love her

My Recipe, For Love:

to have what dreams are made of

when one says, I do

loving as you love yourself

loving that someone

like no one else

Insatiable:

You have become all I want
my love to be

temptation has me wanting
the pleasures of you

being the yes
to all you want to do
now that I
have you   Insatiable

The Hunger:

I am a love strong a house and a home
the everything you think of
leading to I do
when passion says I want to
when passion says
it's you
speaking to
the moments of your dreams

The Things That Lovers Do:

I will love you with intentions

my destination

finding another like mind

call it

what you want

call it

a love that will never part

call it

the things that lovers do

Off Paper:

my thoughts

never saying no

living like I dream

your love be my everything

not just saying I do

imagining my surrender

being the moments

you come

The Lyrical Expressions

become the words of
my imagination

the thoughts

of complicated passions

these
lyrical expressions

Chronicles, Of Passion:

My mind free
penning
your love
could be mine
taking chances
painting emotions
as if it were
my life

Love, And The, Conversation:

the moment to fill
your heart
one-word next line
the passions private collection
saying something beautiful
all the time
foreplay has never been this sweet
sharing whenever
you want to

Mischievous:

Thinking of you
I've got the Dark Man blues
those moments when
I can silhouette your imagination
your lips wet
let me cap that
whispering may I please
be the yes

when love goes right

Captured

she said she loved me

I was moved   a love of the same mind

my attention lured

she captured my emotions as if

she knew my dreams

the reflection was as though

she, were the skin, I'm in

embracing her flow

was to rule this tempest

my heart beating passion

she became the whispers

dwelling in the pleasures of my soul

the sensuality would take me

this body of tenderness birth my desire

leaving me to become   the passion

in this pen

from the book The Lyrical Expressions 2013

My Next Book

pages

A look ahead:

this season

whatever season you're in

      that's

the weather

i'm forecasting

a metaphor i don't want to miss

your wanting

knowing i'm coming

for the influences

i've made

From the book "My Future Seduction" 2022

The Clone in Me

When I am away
voices in the pillows
echoing last night's memories
tracing imprints
left on
sheets
five in the morning
you feel
the clone in me
my name still
resonating

I'll be reading you when the rain comes

a love poem in the making

Edit Love

It was a moment to ease the wanting
sharing that part of me
word play
be my intention
finding love
became the mission
writing myself into
submission
to have mystery
find me
these pages be
the depth of me
editing our love
into a story

My Next Book

You have become the title of
my next book
all I could think of
was your charm
these simple words
2 love birds 2 love signs
making love too
each other's mind
before a touch before we said
how much
having the smiles say
we do
waiting
to give in
waiting   to begin

The Take

I was all in
out to get it like I was independent
love and me

said her name was
Romance
my last chance

my thoughts
had me caressing tights
trying not to
thinking again I'm about to

dancing
the night away
I could feel
bodies touching no air
damn this ain't fair

Finding Me

Time place my thoughts

searching

this mystery

can you be

      My mind

      decision

      the condition

      got me

wrong turn

U-turn

love maybe

my baby

got me blown

on a hook

      second take

gave me conclusion

the way she

      made me

Your Soul On, Fire

I'll be
waiting

when
your dreams come

when
you whisper
can I be

when
your hunger says
I want you

when
you say

I need you

I will answer

Photo Shop

Picture your love and me
see it like I do
call it dream making
sculpting a masterpiece into submission

my giving in
pleasure mapping your senses

first take

Missing Your Love

the way you wear your hair
the way you fill the air
it's got me
reminiscing

tasting yesterday
thinking about tomorrow
wondering could I
love you deeper

having everyday be
the beginning of my dreams
it's got me calling
to say

I'm missing you

Loves In, Need

I wanted to fill my hunger

as well as my needs

knowing one without the other

would leave me incomplete

I could not allow

persuasion to take me

even though I wanted

giving the mystery

surrounding me

so many

distractions

not falling prey to the conversation

surrendering my affections

knowing my needs

were as much as

my hunger

So Emotional

The thought had me
love that is
wrote it down in a poem
expressing
my charm
the mirror reaction
far beyond my expectations
when she said I do;
answering
my confession

Perfect Love

I was wanting
to put love together
like a puzzle
you know when
everything matches
having it be all the things
you do to me
like using the words
of this poem
saying you got me
whispering all the secret things
you are to me
I be
Day Dreaming

She Wanted

She said she needed me
called me
a distraction
it felt as though she
wanted some
complicated passion
said she wanted to read the book
she had checked out
to truly caress the pages of my heart
said my eyes
were her first thought
wanting to see how deep
the passion could be
beyond the exterior
to capture what the words
were all about

after the whispers

A Lover too A Friend

She said make love to me

knowing

it was something I wanted to do

through all the traffic

I could feel

her whispering

loves danger

her passion that is

I would come to

that change

of mind

she wanted to put me in

her discovering

I was all in

a lover to a friend

calling my name

complicated

Your Love, And Me

I found myself
wanting
overflowed
drowning deep
the journey
my commitment
giving in
to your surrender
making dreams
speaking my daily
routine
hungering
your love and me

You Me And, The Conversation

Love spoke my name

imparting why

I would answer how much

her boldness

consumed me

capturing

my intentions

I was blessed the day I found you

speaking

no one will ever love me

like you

The Secret Of, My Heart

I could feel the wanting
speaking passion
and yes, I had that
secret weapon
defining the moment's
asking, have you ever
loved this way?
surrendering my senses
being that
emotional creature
like Complicated Passions

V Kali

I wanted to write a love poem
tasting the echoes
of her name
to find myself lost in
a heart like mine
her presence left dreams
I remember the name
she called me
into the love poem
she made me

The Poem

she's got me reading her
caught up in the moment
I was trying to drown her in
had me falling in love
as if I were the poem

She Rains

she graced the windows of my soul
leaving interpretations, I never knew
like the earth she was giving and
I fell for her

Rules Of, Engagement

Don't let rules get in the way
making conditions
thinking
you're mission control

no strings attached
on being real

no credit card baby
just a maybe
if you're in

I'm out to get it
like blackjack

Changes

let's have this conversation

no holding back on

taking chances

together we can

define destiny

it's your dreams

I want to be in

when my embrace

calls you to be

the tremble

I surrender too

The Music

She was like music
a love poem
I wanted to taste
over again

Anticipation

I thought for a moment . . .
anticipating
how my love would be
reversing roles
understanding how much
you want me
I shared my heart
my imagination too
writing myself all over you

In, The Night Time

the night and its realities
writing more of
the passions private collection

another chapter
of lyrical expression and

I'm loving it

The Inside Story

I found myself in what was to be
the beginning of everyday my life was meant,
in love and consume

my pleasures a circle unbroken
living the inside story
she was all that for me

the awakening of her dreams
became wanting
I could taste as my own

What Becomes

I am to be everything that becomes her
the joy she breathes fills the air around me

every moment she is to be
are now
the pages of my heart

love in the first degree
the sensuality
passionately speaking romanticism

her dreams are
what becomes me

Hidden Thoughts

I need your love
not just what could be

my confession
even though you
ask me not to

not to tell the world
of my desire

how passion speaks to
who you are?
my . . . Gemini Fire

got me singing
I'll come apart

to be in to you

Like July

Knowing passion, the way I do
finding out how
the river flows . . . is how
I'm going to,
do you
the first take
coming after many dates
I'm all in
loving like forever
wanting
your dreams
sex me
I'll sex, you too
making pleasure go boom
my wanting to storm
the room
call it passion
it's hot

like July

Make Love

she said

imagine my name

being the echo

in your dreams

scripting the kisses of your lips

there, there

and   there

my first my last

a prelude

with no indecision

I just closed my eyes and

the dream   came

true

My;

I wanted to reach out
seem to be the right play
being true to you

to feel your emotions
I needed to share my intentions
wanting your affection

now that you're into this book
read between
these lines

discover the passion

Deep Dream

Somewhere in these pages
you will find me
mapping out dreams
in one word are even the next line
sharing my intentions
love will always be
the conversation
never saying no
to the pleasures
coming alive inside of you
hear my name
as I drown myself
in the room
making love
after poetry

A Figment Of, My Imagination

It felt like an illusion beckoning

no doubt she had intentions

speaking in a moment of passion

was she a figment of my imagination?

like a dream

that never happens and yet

there you are

calling me out as if

you want this confession

forget the question

become the answer

be my imagination

Nightcap, The Unwritten Moments

I was night capping

for dreams

the foreplay I wanted to be

she read to me

the edge of her tongue

captured

the unwritten moments of my affections

I was about to live dreams

the moments of my surrender

passionately whispering

like she knew me

called me a nightcap

because I was wanting to get that

mapping out her love like

I just discovered it

reciting

can we come again

The Conversation

I so wanted to share

my convictions

so . . . tempting

my emotions

thinking

last chance

you see

they been waiting on me

to spit like

I'm The Last Poet

sometimes complicated

my emotions

dropping hints

like . . . I'm

out to get this

24

You set my soul
I'm ready
days nights
I got this
being the moments
I'm about to
work this
scripting these affections
all over
your love mine
capturing
the dreams
your eyes
are telling me

Making Love In, Dimensions

loving you like a poem
echoing pleasures
penning dreams

to tempt you
here's to making love
in dimensions

having my confession
every morning after your dreams
without assumptions

Taking Love, For Granted

Love was out to give me something
I could hold on to
as if my life depended on it
thinking conquest
trying to make change
out of nothing
love was something
not to be played

a heart without a gift
an empty box
of pleasures
I couldn't fill
seeing I have nothing
left to give
being taken for granted

Dream Making

crushing the mystery
no second guessing
sharing the
simple things
I think about
you're being my constant daily reminder
of how beautiful love is
embracing serenity

Love Suggestion

taste this

oral translation

let's, count the times

six

nine

yours

mine

Your Love

I've been dreaming confessions
embracing on sheets no covers
it's gone be sexy
like   June
summer love and you
my wanting no ends

I ma do this until the love runs out
drowning 2 love signs
loving like one mind
these pleasures got me thinking
of some dope lines
chasing the whispers of my name

coming like summer love again when
you need me this is how we will get it in
you, being the last
love poem I pen

The State Of, Union

expression have become the norm

how love use to be

what love should be

excepting the will of another

when others are thinking

what's the point of a love poem?

illusions without metaphors

throwing shade wanting to dress up love

clearly needing an intervention

so many distraction

falling prey to attractions

having a truck stop in place of a home

a fake sense of completion

being played in a game called seasons

first thought . . . perception

being true to self

not taking love for granted

giving what you ask for when

surrendering your affections

becoming a union instead of a weekend

Wanting

Wanting
is everything
coming
alive
inside of you
so deep
I never want
to let go

Every Time It Rains

painting
the moment
a bedroom caressed
being touch
by the rain

Wishing

You were that whisper
singing love songs
your body next to mine
before this touched

                    after reading how much
                        your anticipating
                adding another day to the week
                        to have more of you
                    chasing the night away

no interruptions just some
complicated passions
when you are wanting
more than a maybe

                    having me love you like crazy
                        seeing once
                        will never be
                        enough

Have You Ever Called Love?

I am embraced by
the surrender you want to be
without speaking
these kisses
endlessly seeking
the memories
you have never been
you only need to
call me

Under, The Blue Moon

She was that blue moon

my last chance
to romance
the night away

her love my desire

had me photo shopping
giving in
to the mystery

knowing I was a sucker

wanting to
make the fantasy
my reality

gave me reason

.com 4 love

Love.com
discovering places
I want to be
confessing my love deep
sharing your dreams
loving you
to the edge

I'll be waiting

Love:
and Me

love and me
would have the conversation
inviting . . . temptation   you see
anticipation had a thought
commitment said
hold up
asking questions like
are you ready?
my emotions
took a step back
could this be my dreams?
desire whispered
I'm all in
wanting said it's about to be
a sin and then
my heart would speak
saying I don't wont
to lose   asking
who's keeping score
me

Loves Got Me

This Aries fire

my pursuit

out too get it

my life's mission

dream lover thing

knowing its

got me

wanting

to end a well written story

finding that

perfect balance

making the

impossible

possible

A Soup Called Love

Imagine creating love
picture the recipe
. . . I have
the moment I became
Complicated Passions
playing the role of
Doctor Fantastic
work playing on a remedy
sharing the emotions of
Mister Mystery
my concept
everybody wants to be me
don't misinterpret
my analogue
check out the similarities
imagine this being you
loving without
condition

A Conversation, With Love

If love could speak
would it call out to me
if it were   me
I would have the
conversation
sharing the reasons
why it's you
speaking too how   you
make my day
if I were love
I would give purpose to
your smile
I would begin with
the reflection in my eyes
having
this conversation
if I were
speaking
to love

Taken

a shared moment
those of a stranger
words spoken
truth and
dare
understanding
how important it is
to be real
with self
having no illusions when
speaking of
my affection
being taken by a love of my own
becoming that surrender
tuned to my,
future seduction

Writing Thoughts

Painting this page
an illustration
casting it as
my point of view
Dark Man Blues
my understanding
will always be
speaking loves desire
to have passion
be the fire
I surrender to
having no secrets
from you

365

My love
it's got me
tempted
seeking surrender
from another
giving thought to
my intentions
having yes
be the answer when
you hunger
taking your dreams like
I own them

She, Be

She caught my attention
read me like a book
she couldn't put down
I wanted to feel
the movement in
her mind
as she had in mine
putting the words   back together
              to become this next line
her pleasures

Irie Eyes

Emotions got me
I'm in to you
check the reflection
the eyes I see
have been put to paper
love being you
my affections run deep
the pages they speak
saying these are the moments
your love could be
when you are
wanting like me
don't hesitate to read again
and experience
the mystery

The Shadows

It would be a room with a view
imprinting the
impressions of passion
the whispers
my name yours too

the shadows would echo
our affections
I see you

Now That 2 Makes 1

moments of passion
becoming dreams
yours mine
when 2 becomes 1
seeing you're a love poem
from the extension
of my mind
leaving thoughts
inside of you
having it be the what
we come too
picture the reality
your name in ecstasy
sharing the pleasures
of your company
your place my place

The Mix

I be loving you
more than the stars
love the night
I'm about to paint
this masterpiece
your loving me
natures plan
surrendering like
the waves on the shore
coming deeper
you see I just can't
give you up
being the Gumbo File
in my favorite dish
call it a
Creole mix

Mister Mystery

I am a love called deep
the bloodline in me
a mystery
French Creole African too
a, pleasure mix
of Gumbo treats
a complicated passionate freak
some of the names
you can call me
my love home grow
season to please
you can have all of me
once bitten
your love will be
drowning in mystery
let's make it
a special occasion
this recipe

your love and me deep

you can underline all the moments you want
I'm the one for you
think about it

I'll be that dare you've dreamed
we can turn love out
you got kisses I've got kisses too
here there yes there

call me what you want
I'll never say no
I'll put all the locks on the door
if you want you can keep score

I'll give in
If you let me do it again
temptation is my name
whisper me

Candlelight: And you

The moment was set
or should I say
the mood
sweet music wine candle light
then you
sweet harmony
had me
. . . on a song
I want you
the reflection a bedtime story
reading to a love poem
soul searching on a mystery
making love
to your mind
one word
this next line
you need to give in
whispering my name
before and after
this kiss

Another Day, With Love

I had a date . . . love came calling

She was like the rain

natures blessing

all I ever wanted, and I was wanting

I imagine the moment

my boldness became surrender

she was that roadmap

to my destiny and I knew it

I could never say no

to the sun

having her every morning after

would give me

another day

with love

The Keys Of, Passion

I be chasing harmony
it's a love thing
I be making dreams
always wanting
before never
the realness
I've got her singing in key
Doctor Fantastic
it's me
having whispers
come true
from the mention of my name
dropping hints
as if I were
complicated passions
here's a line
I'll be tempting temptation
making dares reality
just to give you
more of me

Eyes

She called out to me
a reflection
I would drown in
sharing my affection
expressing my thoughts
of temptation
loving her hair . . .
loving the picture painted
in the clothes she wears
taken by the
sensual smile
the caress of her hips
softly against mine
to drown deep
into a kiss
my eyes
picturing the moments
I would miss

Exit Left

Caught up in a moment of
thinking I could have
everything
seems I was taking love
for granted
speaking my confession
making stop signs
my protection
always on the look out
for temptation
never wanting to give in
knowing I had an exit
in my pen
never surrendering to the passion
I would drown them in
love and me
expressing my affections
leaving photos
of my imagination
making love to your mind . . . thinking
about that exit

JZ

She spoke to my;
presentation
me speaking about love
sharing truth about
my flow
saying they don't know
left me with
a smile
the thought priceless
I could only pay
homage
being real to myself
I stayed true
to my pen . . . I would never give in
to be sound like
someone else
no second guessing
living myself
having fun
being real with it
speaking
Complicated Passions

If I Ever Had You

I've shared my imagination
imagining
was it more I could do . . . to
get your attention
wanting had me
I needed to come with
a different view
understanding no one loves like I want you
read my temptation
hear it in
the conversation
me sharing the moments
of my dreams
whispering
what your love means to me
knowing you're
wanting the mystery
of a love to be
if I had you
I would share in all the things
you want to do
let's call it . . . Dark Man Blues

2019

my next book

leaves me . . . tempted

asking of myself

can you give more of this?

with your pen

sweet moments of getting it in

this word that word

some dope lines

complicated passions on my mind

giving instructions

taking them too

damn just my imagination

coming alive

roleplaying with intentions

dream chasing

making statements

you are the

conversation

my wanting that

forever recipe for love

having it be   just

you

Read

I would read her
because it felt good
true story
I was taken
by this life
I wanted more and
she was giving
invited me like
welcome home
she took my emotions
leaving echoes
even the walls would remember
her name
is poetry

From the book "Mischievous" 2021

Coming in 2020

Mister Mystery

Everybody Publishing

Reading You

Innated Divinity

Dark Man Blues

"The Series"

Innated Divinity

The Wrong Side, Of Time

My life became an illusion

printed words were now the reality

my thoughts

penned from

my dreams

being a product of

my age

painting into loves mystery

she would consume me

without condition

knowing she

had my pen daily

my thoughts

whispers on paper

she gave

life back to me

her name . . . her name is

poetry

Bonus:

Mister Mystery

I speak of these moments
in every breath I take
that manifestation you wish for
even your fantasy
my words bleed expression
when the coming of your love falls
I will fill your well
with a kiss to remember
when your lips are surrendering
to the tales of
Mister Mystery

Form the book "Mister Mystery" 2020

uncharted memories

she was like a moving violation I needed to ticket
she thought she knew it all
wanting me after a kiss

I charged in I had to have this
it would be a crime not to
being exposed like I was I couldn't look away

fixed on points I wanted to discover
I was about to map my way to the moon
locked in rocket love

my daily routine

I've dreamed you
first encounter my only
that chance when I am under your skin
whispering take me
as I capture you being
the echoes of my name

that's the way

The clone in me

I am that mystery lost

in your dreams   that tomorrow

you wake to   when

I am away   the

voice in the pillows

echoing last night's memories

tracing imprints

left on

sheets

five in the morning

you feel

the clone in me

my name still

resonating

an undisclosed location

have a Conversation
with love

www.ingramcontent.com/pod-product-compliance
Lightning Source LLC
Chambersburg PA
CBHW030339020726
47493CB00004B/1339